The
Columbus Story

The

Pictures by
LEO POLITI

Columbus Story

By ALICE DALGLIESH

Charles Scribner's Sons

New York

DISCARD

6/78 WLS 4.17

JB
C

38421

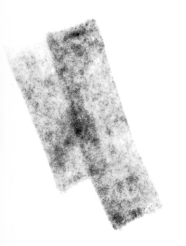

13 15 17 19 21 23 25 27 29 RD/C 30 28 26 24 22 20 18 16 14 12

Copyright 1955 by Alice Dalgliesh and Leo Politi

PRINTED IN THE UNITED STATES OF AMERICA

ISBN 684-13179-X

AUTHOR'S NOTE

In making this book the artist and I have selected those events in the life of Columbus which seem to be most interesting to children. The narrative, planned for reading aloud, is historical, with legends omitted, and the Admiral's own words are used as refrains. I believe even small children can appreciate the dignity of this. To keep the narrative simple, only a few characters are introduced; only a few names used.

Older children may like to know that Ferdinand Columbus, years afterwards, wrote some of the proudest words ever written by a son about a father. In his copy of Seneca's plays there was a prophecy that some day a great new continent would be discovered. Beside this Ferdinand wrote:

THIS PROPHECY WAS FULFILLED BY MY FATHER, THE ADMIRAL, IN THE YEAR 1492

Of the many thousands of words written about the Discovery none are more dramatic than these.

I wish to thank Little, Brown and Company for permission to use two lines of the young sailor's song at dawn from *Admiral of the Ocean Sea* by Samuel Eliot Morison.

I am also indebted to Barnes and Noble, Inc., for permission to use several direct quotes from the diary of Columbus in *The Northmen, Columbus and Cabot*.

A Boy and the Sea

Once there was a boy who loved the sea. He lived in the town of Genoa in Italy and his name was Christopher Columbus.

Christopher was the son of a weaver. Every day he could see his father and mother weaving cloth. But, although he helped his father, Christopher didn't want to be a weaver. He wanted to be a sailor and go to sea.

Whenever he could, he went to the wharves to see the big ships coming and going. The sailors told stories of their adventures—stories that were true, and partly true and some that were not true at all. Christopher listened. Christopher wondered.

The sea around Genoa was blue and beautiful. But far away, so the sailors said, there was the Sea of Darkness. No one knew

much about this sea, or ocean. No one knew much about the lands beyond it.

The sailors told of strange creatures that lived in the Sea of Darkness. Sail on it and you took your life in your hands. At any time a huge sea serpent or an enormous fish might rise up out of the ocean. One of these creatures might even swallow your ship. It was full of mystery, full of danger—this Sea of Darkness.

Mystery, danger, adventure—what exciting words! Christopher wanted more than ever to be a sailor. The wind that ruffled his red hair seemed to call to him, "Come!"

"Come, come, come!" The waves that lapped the wharves said it over and over.

"Adventure, adventure, adventure!" The white sails of ships said it again and again. And over and over, again and again, Christopher wished for adventure.

As Christopher grew older, he read books about the wonderful countries across the ocean. One of these was a book written by Marco Polo, a man who had traveled to the countries we now call India and China and Japan.

Adventure Begins

As Christopher read, he let the words of the book make pictures in his mind. Bright pictures, magical pictures of lands called India, Cathay, Cipango. Cathay was ruled over by a great king. There were gardens and flowers and palaces with roofs of gold. In that country there were jewels and spices. The birds sang sweetly....

Christopher Columbus dreamed as he read.

But he did not only dream of adventure—he worked hard to get ready for it. He studied maps, and learned how to make them. He found out all he could about the sea and sailing—and he went to sea many times.

Once the ship in which Christopher was sailing sank. Christopher held on to a piece of board and floated ashore. He was in the country of Portugal. This was a country with many sailors and fine ships, so Christopher decided to live there. After a time he married and had a son named Diego.

In Portugal, Columbus learned more about the sea. The Portuguese and Spanish captains had sailed out into the ocean and found islands. Columbus sailed to some of the islands, and heard that the people living there believed that there were more islands farther on.

In Portugal, Columbus also made maps and sold them. He talked to other map makers and men who knew about the world. Once men had thought that the world was flat—but now many people knew that it was round.

So—if Columbus sailed to the East, as everyone did, he would get to Japan and India. But—if he sailed to the West as no one did, wouldn't he get there, too? If he was going to try it, he had to have ships and sailors and money. He went to the King of Portugal. The king listened but said No.

Columbus knew he must find another country that would help him. What about Spain? Diego's mother had died, so Columbus took his five-year-old son with him to Spain. There he left him at a monastery, with some kind monks who would teach him. Then Columbus went to Ferdinand and Isabella, King and Queen of Spain.

He told them of wonderful countries across the ocean and of gold and jewels and spices. He would tell the people who lived in these countries about God. If only he had money and ships. . . .

The King and Queen listened but said No.

For six long years Columbus hoped the King and Queen would help him. He lived part of the time in Cordoba, the city where the King and Queen had their palace. Here he had another son, Ferdinand. Ferdinand's mother was Spanish.

Columbus was tired and sad. He did not have much money. No one would listen to his plans, and now the great adventure seemed very far away.

Diego was still at the monastery, so Columbus went to visit him. One of the monks knew the Queen, and he asked her to listen to Columbus. The Queen sent Columbus a mule to ride and money to buy new clothes. He rode back to tell his story all over again. After a time the King and Queen said they would help him. They gave him the fine title, "Admiral of the Ocean Sea."

The Admiral Sails

With the help of the King and Queen, Columbus was able to get three ships. They were the *Niña*, the *Pinta* and the *Santa Maria*.

The three ships sailed from Spain on a Friday in the month of August in the year 1492. The sailors thought it was unlucky to sail on a Friday. Perhaps they would never come back to their homes in Spain. Columbus had faith that he would come back to his two little sons. He left them in the city of Cordoba to go to school while he was away.

Out into the Sea of Darkness sailed the *Niña*, the *Pinta* and the *Santa Maria*. Columbus was on the largest ship, the *Santa Maria*. He was the leader, Christopher Columbus, Admiral of the Ocean Sea.

Columbus said that he would write in a book all the things that happened. This would keep him busy day and night. "I shall forget sleep," said the Admiral.

On and on sailed the *Niña*, the *Pinta* and the *Santa Maria*.

The rudder of the *Pinta* broke loose, and she was not steering well. So the ships stopped at the Canary Islands to mend the rudder. There they also gave the *Niña* a new set of sails, so she could go more swiftly.

On and on they sailed, with the swift *Niña* and *Pinta* ahead. On and on! The sailors began to be more and more afraid. They wanted to go back to Spain. Columbus was sure that the countries they were looking for must be near. He had made a mistake about the size of the world, however. He thought it was smaller than it was, and did not know how far they must sail.

On and on—day after day after day, watching for signs that land was near. Birds in the sky, seaweed on the sea, whales spouting, fish leaping—but no land. Nothing but sea—and sea—and sea.

The sailors grew more frightened and more angry.

"I trust in God that soon we shall sight land," said the Admiral.

On and on sailed the *Niña*, the *Pinta* and the *Santa Maria*.

Now they saw land birds, a board, and a branch with berries floating on the water. Land must be near.

Everyone hoped to be the first to see the wonderful country. The King and Queen had promised a reward to the one who first saw land. It was like a race. The *Pinta* and the *Niña* were sailing swiftly ahead. Near morning the captain of the *Pinta* thought he saw land. He fired a cannon to tell the news to the other ships.

Land! Land! Land! Up into the rigging, up the masts went the sailors, climbing, climbing—higher—higher—higher, to see into the distance.

On the *Santa Maria* the Admiral knelt and thanked God. And now everyone began to sing. The sound of the singing went from one ship to another across the water: "Glory to God in the highest! Glory to God."

But when the sun rose there was no land, only clouds and the sea smooth and quiet as a river.

"Watch well for land," said the Admiral.

The New World

On and on sailed the *Niña*, the *Pinta* and the *Santa Maria*.

And one night Columbus thought he saw a light in the darkness—a small light like a wax candle. It was a sailor on the *Pinta* who first saw land, but Columbus claimed the reward for first seeing a light.

Again the sound of song went from one ship to another.

They had to wait for daylight. The hours went slowly . . . slowly. Then daylight came swiftly into the sky, like the lifting of a curtain on a play. This *was* land. And on the beach were people. . . .

A boy sailor sang as he did every morning:

> . . . *Blessed be the light of day*
> *And He who sends the night away.*

The Admiral went ashore in a boat, carrying the royal flag of Spain. The captains of the *Niña* and the *Pinta* went ashore in other boats carrying the ships' banners with a green cross and a crown.

They landed on the sandy shore. The Admiral said that the island now belonged to the King and Queen of Spain. He called the island San Salvador, meaning Holy Savior.

Now both the island people and the men on the ships saw strange things for the first time.

The brown island people saw three big "canoes" with white sails. These canoes were so lovely that they must have come down from the sky. Did not all good things come from the sky? They ran from house to house saying: "Come! Come to see the people from Heaven."

And here were men with strange light-colored skins. Their bodies were all covered with cloth in colors as beautiful as the feathers of birds. They came with gifts. There were small pieces of metal that made a tinkling sound. Chug! Chug! said the brown people, trying to make a sound like bells. There were beads as bright as the white men's clothes and pieces of red cloth to wear on the head. . . .

These things the island people saw with wonder and delight.

Columbus and his men saw a new beautiful world.

Here were brown men with no clothes at all. Their bodies were painted red and other bright colors. Could this be India, these people Indians? Columbus gave them that name, though this was not India. They came to the ships in canoes, or swimming, with gifts of cotton and parrots and food. They were pleased to take gifts of bells and beads and scarlet caps. They were a gentle and friendly people.

And on the island there were palm trees and trees so tall they seemed to reach the sky. It was the twelfth day of October, but these trees had not lost their leaves. They were as green and beautiful as the trees of Spain in the month of May.

"It is a glory to look upon them. My eyes will never tire of such loveliness, nor my ears of listening to the songs of birds," said the Admiral.

On and on sailed the *Niña*, the *Pinta* and the *Santa Maria*.

They sailed from island to island and each one seemed lovelier than the other. The trees and flowers smelled so delicious, the birds sang so sweetly! The people lived in "pretty houses, full of tame birds" and had "dogs that never barked."

At that time men who discovered new countries always thought their own way of living was the best.

"We must teach these people to wear clothes and teach them our ways," said the Admiral.

Here were beautiful lands—but where was the gold and where the spices? Gold and spices—gold and spices—the words kept going through the Admiral's head. He could not go back to Spain without the riches he had promised to find.

Where is the gold? the Admiral wondered. He showed the island people gold and he showed them spices—cinnamon, nutmeg and sweet-smelling cloves.

Always they told him in sign language that these things were on another island—over there—farther on.

So on and on sailed the *Niña*, the *Pinta* and the *Santa Maria*. After a time the captain of the *Pinta* sailed off and left the other ships. Perhaps he wanted the gold and spices for himself. Perhaps he remembered that Columbus had claimed the reward for first seeing land.

Soon the *Niña* and the *Santa Maria* came to a big island with tall mountains. It was a beautiful island and the trees were still green, although it was almost Christmas time.

Columbus thought this must be Japan, but it was another big island called Haiti. There was a great king, or chief, on this island. There was some gold, but no fine palaces with gold roofs.

Now there was a great exchanging of presents. The Indians came with cotton cloth, small pieces of gold, parrots—and even three fat geese. They came to the ships in many, many canoes, bringing bread and fish and jars of fresh water. Hundreds of them swam to the ships. By this time some of the sailors were giving the Indians almost anything—even bits of colored glass. The Admiral told them this was not the right thing to do.

As the next day would be Christmas, Columbus planned to go ashore and have a big Christmas festival. Everyone in the island would come. The first Christmas in the New World would be a wonderful day. . . .

These had been busy days on the ship with so many Indians coming to visit. Columbus was tired, but the *Santa Maria* must sail to the part of the island where the chief lived.

On Christmas Eve he went to his cabin to sleep. A young sailor was allowed to steer the *Santa Maria*—and ran it on the rocks. Then the ship began to leak, and fell over on her side. Columbus and his men went to the *Niña* by boat.

So Christmas Day was not a holiday—it was a working day. Everyone worked hard to take food and water and goods from the *Santa Maria* to the *Niña*. The Indians helped, and even the chief of the island came to watch. When he saw what had happened he was sad.

Columbus invited the chief to dinner on board the *Niña*. Then the king invited Columbus and his men to have another meal on the island. The Indian chief wore, very proudly, a shirt and gloves Columbus had given him.

Home to Spain

Early in the new year, the *Pinta* came back to join the *Niña*. Columbus left some men to build a town on the island—and the *Niña* and the *Pinta* sailed back to Spain.

Back across the Sea of Darkness sailed the two small ships on a sea that became rough and stormy. At times the Admiral, like everyone else, was afraid. He thought of his little sons in Cordoba, so he wrote a letter to the King and Queen and sealed it up in a wooden barrel. The letter told about the New World and also asked the King and Queen to take care of Diego and Ferdinand. The barrel, Columbus thought, would drift ashore.

"I put all my trust in God," said the Admiral. "He has been with me on my voyage and He will be with me now."

The *Niña* was a good, seaworthy ship and she came safely through the storm. The *Pinta* reached Spain first, and the captain tried to see the King and Queen. They would not see him, for they were waiting until the Admiral himself arrived.

When at last Columbus reached Spain, he went first to see his sons. Then he went to the King and Queen to tell them of the lands he had found. He took with him some Indians he had brought on the ship.

Great crowds came to watch the procession. Ferdinand and Diego must have been proud. Their father—yes, that important and brave man was their father—Christopher Columbus, Admiral of the Ocean Sea.

When the time of celebration was over, there was work to be done. There was more to be found out about the wonderful New World across the ocean.

So Columbus sailed again. This time there were seventeen ships with flags and banners flying.

On shore, crowds of people cheered and waved as the ships sailed out into the ocean. Diego and Ferdinand stood watching as their father's ships went out on another exciting adventure. Some day Ferdinand would go with him.

The Admiral sailed four times and came back four times. Twice he or his men landed on the mainland. He never really knew that he had discovered the big country that is now called America. He did know that he had found a large piece of land.

So every year on the twelfth of October—and many other times—we think of Columbus and listen to his story. Then as we listen, we seem to see him standing on the deck of his ship, the wind blowing through his white hair. And we can almost hear him say:

"Watch well for land. Watch well for land."

DISCARD

38421

J
B COLUMBUS
DALGLIESH
   COLUMBUS STORY